HIP-HOP

Hip-Hop

Eminem

Joanne Mattern

MC
PUBLISHERS

Mason Crest Publishers

Eminem

FRONTIS Eminem displays his characteristic attitude as he walks on stage to accept the Video of the Year award at the MTV Video Music Awards, 2002.

PRODUCED BY 21ST CENTURY PUBLISHING AND COMMUNICATIONS, INC.

MASON CREST PUBLISHERS INC.
370 Reed Road
Broomall, Pennsylvania 19008
(866)MCP-BOOK (toll free)
www.masoncrest.com

Printed in Malaysia.

9 8 7 6 5 4 3 2

Library of Congress Cataloging-in-Publication Data

Mattern, Joanne, 1963–
    Eminem / Joanne Mattern.
        p. cm. — (Hip-hop)
    Includes bibliographical references (p.   ) and index.
ISBN-13: 978-1-4222-0118-3
ISBN-10: 1-4222-0118-X
1. Eminem (Musician)—Juvenile literature. 2. Rap musicians—United States—Biography—Juvenile literature. I. Title. II. Series.
ML3930.E46M38 2006
782.421649092—dc22
[B]   2006011855

Publisher's notes:
- All quotations in this book come from original sources, and contain the spelling and grammatical inconsistencies of the original text.

- The Web sites mentioned in this book were active at the time of publication. The publisher is not responsible for Web sites that have changed their addresses or discontinued operation since the date of publication. The publisher will review and update the Web site addresses each time the book is reprinted.

Contents

Hip-Hop Timeline

1974 Hip-hop pioneer Afrika Bambaataa organizes the Universal Zulu Nation.

1988 *Yo! MTV Raps* premieres on MTV.

1970s Hip-hop as a cultural movement begins in the Bronx, New York City.

1985 *Krush Groove*, a hip-hop film about Def Jam Recordings, is released featuring Run-D.M.C., Kurtis Blow, LL Cool J, and the Beastie Boys.

1970s DJ Kool Herc pioneers the use of breaks, isolations, and repeats using two turntables.

1979 The Sugarhill Gang's song "Rapper's Delight" is the first hip-hop single to go gold.

1986 Run-D.M.C. are the first rappers to appear on the cover of *Rolling Stone* magazine.

1970

1980

1988

1976 Grandmaster Flash & the Furious Five pioneer hip-hop MCing and freestyle battles.

1986 Beastie Boys' album *Licensed to Ill* is released and becomes the best-selling rap album of the 1980s.

1970s Break dancing emerges at parties and in public places in New York City.

1982 Afrika Bambaataa embarks on the first European hip-hop tour.

1988 Hip-hop music annual record sales reaches $100 million.

1970s Graffiti artist Vic pioneers tagging on subway trains in New York City.

1984 *Graffiti Rock*, the first hip-hop television program, premieres.

1993 Rapper Snoop Dogg's album *Doggystyle* is the first debut album to hit the music charts at number one.

2006 Queen Latifah becomes the first hip-hop artist to receive a star on the Hollywood Walk of Fame.

1989 DJ Jazzy Jeff & The Fresh Prince become the first hip-hop artists to win a Grammy Award.

2003 Rapper Eminem becomes the first hip-hop artist to win an Academy Award.

2005 Hip-hop artist Kanye West appears on the cover of *Time* magazine.

1989 Rap is added as a new category to the *Billboard* charts.

1997 East Coast rapper Notorious B.I.G. (aka Biggie Smalls) is murdered.

2004 First National Hip-Hop Political Convention is held in Newark, New Jersey.

1989   **2000**   **2006**

1990s Hip-hop emerges in Europe.

1996 West Coast rapper Tupac Shakur is shot and killed.

2005 Rapper Will Smith opens the Philadelphia Live 8 concert as part of 10 simultaneous concerts held worldwide to bring attention to the extreme poverty in Africa.

1989 First gangsta rap album, *Straight Outta Compton*, is released by N.W.A.

2001 The hip-hop political action group, Hip-Hop Summit Action Network, is founded by Russell Simmons.

2006 The Smithsonian Institute National Museum of American History announces the creation of a new hip-hop exhibition scheduled to open in three to five years.

1992 Dr. Dre's album *The Chronic* is released; it redefines West Coast rap.

Eminem appears at the world premiere of his movie *8 Mile* **in Westwood Village, Los Angeles. The rapper made Academy Awards history when his song won an Oscar for Best Original Song from a Motion Picture.**

8 Mile

When the Academy Award nominations for Best Original Song from a Motion Picture were announced early in 2003, there was one song that stood out from the other nominees. That song was "Lose Yourself" from the film *8 Mile*. The star of that movie, and the composer and performer of the song, was **controversial** hip-hop superstar Eminem.

8 Mile told the story of a young man growing up on the rough streets of Detroit and his struggle to achieve his dream of becoming a hip-hop performer. The movie starred Eminem and was based closely on his life. However, it was not an autobiography. Eminem played a character named Jimmy "Rabbit" Smith. Like Eminem, Jimmy came from a poor, troubled family. Like Eminem, Jimmy was obsessed with hip-hop and saw the music world as a way out of his dead-end existence in the Detroit slums. However, unlike Eminem, Jimmy suffered terrible stage fright, which made it seem like his dream could never happen.

When it was released in November 2002, *8 Mile* was a success, both with critics and at the box office. Film reviewer James Berardinelli echoed the feelings of many critics when he wrote:

> **"Formulaic movies can work if they are well-made, and *8 Mile* qualifies. . . . From an acting standpoint, the real question is whether Eminem can carry a movie. The fact that the screenplay for *8 Mile* is semi-autobiographical helps; it doesn't require the star to stretch his range too far. Nevertheless, Eminem acquits himself admirably. He understands that acting isn't all words and gestures; it involves body language and eye contact."**

The soundtrack featured many of Eminem's previous songs as well as new tracks written specifically for the project. One of these new songs was "Lose Yourself."

A Surprising Choice

The nomination of "Lose Yourself" for an Academy Award was a great surprise. The Oscars are the most important awards in Hollywood, and many people were stunned that a hip-hop song was even considered for this honor, given its explicit content.

The nomination of "Lose Yourself" was also a surprise because of Eminem himself. By 2003 he had become a hip-hop superstar. Although Eminem had many fans, he also had many enemies. Many parents and other authority figures were horrified by the **graphic** words to his songs, which were filled with **profanity** and glorified violence against women and homosexuals. Eminem's anger and violence were also a problem in his personal life. He had been arrested for **assault** and had a violent and troubled relationship with his wife. These were not the qualities normally associated with Academy Award nominees, and some wondered what kind of message the nomination was sending.

Eminem Says No

At all previous Academy Award shows, the nominated songs were performed live on television, usually by the person who had recorded them. Gil Cates, the **producer** of the Academy Awards, told Eminem that he would not be allowed to perform the original **lyrics** of "Lose Yourself" on television because they contained too much profanity. Instead, he was asked to sing an edited, cleaned-up version.

Eminem refused and told Cates that he would not even attend the award ceremony. Ultimately, Cates decided that "Lose Yourself" would not be performed at all during the show. "There's no rule that the nominees have to sing or that you even have to include all of the numbers in the show," he told reporters.

Rapper Eminem performs his hit "Lose Yourself" at the 45th annual Grammy Awards on February 23, 2003, in New York. One month later, the song won him the first Oscar ever awarded to a rap song.

Luis Resto poses with the Oscar for "Lose Yourself" for Best Song. He cowrote the song with Eminem and was on hand to accept the award. Resto is a keyboard player who has worked with Eminem on several albums.

On March 23, 2003, the Academy Awards were held in Los Angeles. Nominees for the Best Original Song were announced. Along with "Lose Yourself" from *8 Mile*, the nominees included "The Hands That Built America" from the historical drama *Gangs of New York*, "Father and Daughter" from the animated feature *The Wild Thornberrys Movie*, "Burn it Blue" from the biopic *Frida*, and "I Move On" from the musical *Chicago*. And the winner was . . . "Lose Yourself"!

Luis Resto, who cowrote the song with Eminem, picked up the award. It was the first rap song to win an Oscar. Although Eminem did not show up to claim his award, a representative from his record company announced that the rapper "is always thankful when the work he puts into his music is recognized by others." Backstage, Resto told reporters, "It means a lot to him, believe me, this means a whole lot to him. I just don't think he expected it."

The fact that the original version of "Lose Yourself" was not allowed to be performed on television yet went on to win an Academy Award perfectly summed up Eminem's life, work, and relationship to authority. He has sold millions of records, won numerous music industry awards, and been praised by fans and critics for his lyrics that explore the darker side of life. He is seen as a master in his field. And yet he cannot escape scorn and anger from many people over his **brutal** lyrics and bad-boy attitude. He excels at saying what people do not want to hear.

Eminem has broken many barriers in his quest to be taken seriously as a white artist in the black world of hip-hop. He has risen far above his humble, difficult beginnings and reached the heights of stardom. Through all the ups and downs of a **turbulent** life and career, Eminem has always managed to come out on top.

Marshall Mathers, also known as Eminem, poses in front of a graffiti-covered wall. Much of his early life was spent in poor neighborhoods in the Detroit area, and Marshall attended many different schools during his childhood.

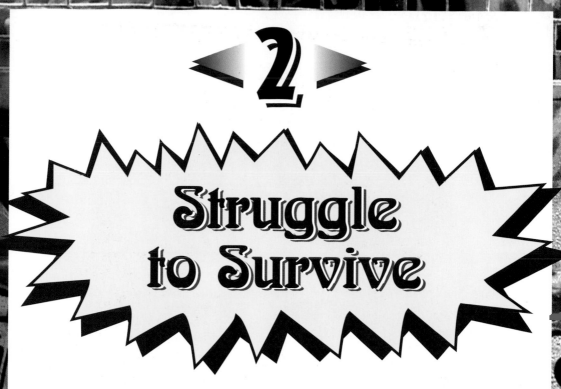

Struggle to Survive

Marshall Bruce Mathers III, who would gain fame as the rapper Eminem, was born on October 17, 1972, in St. Joseph, Missouri. Marshall's mother, Debbie, was only 17 when he was born. His father, Marshall Bruce Mathers II, was 24. The couple had married two years earlier, when Debbie was just 15.

While Marshall was still an infant, the family moved to North Dakota so his father could take a job as the assistant manager of a hotel. However, there were problems between Debbie and her husband. Debbie often complained about his "erratic behavior." When Marshall was about two years old, his mother finally had enough. She took her son and fled back to her mother's home in Missouri. By 1975 the Mathers were divorced.

For the next few years, Debbie worked at a variety of jobs, while little Marshall was cared for by his father's aunt and uncle. "They took care of me a lot," he told *Rolling Stone* magazine. And they gave Marshall the only

As a small boy, Marshall never had a stable home life for any extended period of time. His parents were divorced when he was very young, and after his mother left Missouri and moved to Detroit, his life changed forever.

stable home he had as a child. When he was still young, his mother took him from that home and moved him to Michigan. For the next few years, they lived in and around the city of Detroit.

On the Edge of Society

Debbie and Marshall never had much money, so they could not afford to live in nice neighborhoods. Instead, they lived in public housing and run-down trailer parks that were one step above the **ghetto**. Eminem told an interviewer, "We kept getting kicked out of every house we were in. I believe six months was the longest we ever lived in a house." Marshall was usually the only white child in these overwhelmingly black neighborhoods. It didn't take him long to pick up the rhythms of black culture and music.

The family moved so much that he attended at least 20 schools during his childhood, which made him a loner. Always being the new kid made him a target for bullies. He recalled to *Rolling Stone*, "Kids are mean to other kids. School is a tough thing to go through."

Trouble at Home

Things were not much better for Marshall at home. At the time his mother was taking two drugs, Vicodin (a painkiller) and Valium (a sedative). Although Debbie had prescriptions for these drugs, Eminem later claimed that she was abusing them. He has also said that Debbie made him believe that he had ADHD (Attention Deficit and Hyperactivity Disorder). She even convinced doctors to give him a prescription for a drug called Ritalin.

While Marshall was growing up, Debbie had a series of boyfriends. One man, named Fred Samra Jr., had a longer relationship with Debbie than most, and the two had a son together named Nathan Samra-Mathers. Marshall later called Nathan's dad "the closest thing I had to a father figure." However, that relationship ended after five years. Debbie had trouble caring for her young son and was later accused of abusing Nathan both emotionally and physically. The courts stepped in, and Debbie lost custody of Nathan, who was sent to a series of foster homes.

Goodbye, High School; Hello, Music

By his teen years, Marshall was living in Warren, a suburb just across 8 Mile Road from Detroit. Most of the time, he lived with his great-grandmother. However, he often visited his mother and younger half-brother, who lived in a trailer park nearby.

When Marshall was 14, he enrolled in Warren's Lincoln High School. However, he had little interest or ability in school. He later told an interviewer, "I failed ninth grade three times, but I don't think it

Eminem's troubled relationship with his mother Debbie was depicted in the movie _8 Mile_. In the film, actress Kim Basinger played Marshall's mother. Debbie Mathers has sued her son for his negative depictions of her in his music.

was necessarily 'cause I'm stupid. I didn't go to school. I couldn't deal." In 1989 he dropped out and never went back to Lincoln High again. Instead, he began working as a cook and dishwasher for $5.50 an hour at Gilbert's Lodge, a family-style restaurant.

Although Marshall did not succeed academically, he did make important musical connections during his years at Lincoln High. He was first introduced to rap through his uncle Ronnie. Although he was Marshall's uncle, Ronnie was only two months older, and the boys were close friends. One day, Ronnie played the rap song "Reckless" by Ice-T from the soundtrack of a movie called _Breakin'_. Marshall was captivated. The early introduction made it easy for him to jump right into the local hip-hop scene in high school. He became part of a group called Soul Intent and often rapped at talent shows in the neighborhood.

Marshall further developed his talent in the basement recording studio of a friend named Mike Ruby. At first, the boys used traditional two-line rhyming couplets, but Marshall soon got bored with this style. He began creating what he called "the inside rhyme." According to friend Jay Fields, this meant he "put as many words that rhymed into a line as he could fit." Marshall was soon showing real lyrical sophistication. During this time he also came up with his stage name, M&M, after his initials.

However, the young rapper could not find many people to listen to his clever rhymes. The hip-hop scene in Detroit was entirely black at that time, and no one wanted to listen to a white boy rap. Instead, Eminem became what is called a "battle MC." A battle MC trades insults with other MCs live on stage. Eminem often appeared at a Detroit music store called the Hip Hop Shop, trading insults and rhymes with anyone who would join him.

This scene from *8 Mile* shows Jimmy during a rap battle against a character named Lotto. Marshall began his real rap career as a battle MC at a small music store in Detroit called the Hip Hop Shop.

One day, a local record producer named Marky Bass heard Marshall rapping and invited him into his recording studio. "He was phenomenal," Bass said. "I dropped everything I was doing and I put everything I had into this kid." In 1996 Bass and Marshall, who had changed his stage name from M&M to Eminem, recorded an album called *Infinite*.

Eminem had high hopes now that he had recorded an album. Unfortunately, no one else was very interested. He sold about 500 copies of *Infinite* out of the trunk of his car. The album was a financial failure. And other rappers claimed that Eminem wasn't doing anything new and fresh. It looked like his musical career was going nowhere.

This photo of Marshall Mathers and Kimberly Ann Scott was taken in the 1990s, before Marshall became famous. His on-again, off-again relationship with Kim would make headlines as they went through a cycle of marriages and divorces.

Eminem and Kim

When he was only 15, Eminem had met a 13-year-old girl named Kimberly Ann Scott at a friend's house. Kimberly had also had a difficult childhood and had just been released from a youth detention house. The two were immediately attracted to each other and began dating.

In 1995, while Eminem was working at Gilbert's Lodge and trying to start a hip-hop career, Kim discovered she was pregnant. The realization that he was about to become a father made Eminem even more desperate to succeed. He wanted to provide for his family and give his daughter the things he'd never had. There was no way he could do that working for minimum wage at a restaurant and living with his mother.

Marshall and Kim's daughter, Hailie Jade Scott, was born on December 25, 1995. Eminem later said that Hailie's birth was the high point of his life. Unfortunately, the joy he felt did not last. When *Infinite* failed to sell in 1996, he went into despair. Although he and Kim loved each other, they broke up, and Kim refused to let Eminem see his newborn daughter. Depressed, the rapper took an overdose of Tylenol and tried to kill himself.

The suicide attempt failed after he threw up the medications. Terrified at what he'd been about to do, Eminem decided to make a new start. He would do his best to succeed as a rapper. He would be a father to his child and start over again with Kim too. Things were about to change in a big way.

Eminem was often worried about how he would support his new family. He worked long hours and hoped for a way to break into music. The lyrical persona of Slim Shady gave Eminem the freedom to create unusual and controversial raps.

3

Slim Shady Finds Success

The mid-1990s brought many changes to Eminem's life. Although he and Kim Scott eventually got back together, he was unable to support his future wife and their newborn child. The couple had to move in with Eminem's mother to save money. Given Eminem's troubled relationship with Debbie, this was not a happy arrangement.

Eminem's dreams of hip-hop success had been shattered by the disappointing failure of *Infinite*. For a time, he even gave up music and worked 60-hour weeks at Gilbert's Lodge in an attempt to pay the bills and support his family. The long hours and family responsibilities left little time for anything else.

The Detroit Music Scene

Being from Detroit made an impact on Eminem's music and style. The city's musical history includes country, blues, jazz, rock, techno, dance, and hip-hop, and Detroit musicians had long combined white and black influences. Legendary music critic Dave Marsh from Pontiac, Michigan, a city just north of Detroit, wrote:

> **"I don't think you can imagine a single white performer from Detroit—from the era of McKinney's Cotton Pickers to today—who didn't want to sound like they were making some kind of African-American music. I don't mean that they wanted to be black, whatever that would mean. I'm talking about the deepest influence for everyone from Mitch Ryder to Johnnie Ray, to Bob Seger, to the Romantics, to Iggy Pop, to the MC5—you name it, it was black music."**

Marsh also pointed out that there was more to Detroit's music scene than its inclusion of African-American influences. Hard rock artists such as Ted Nugent and Grand Funk Railroad, as well as early punk bands like MC5 and the Stooges, all had tough attitudes. Eminem followed in the tradition of blurring racial lines and soon added his own spin to the Detroit bad-boy attitude.

By the 1990s the city was home to a vibrant underground hip-hop scene. Detroit's rappers borrowed from the very different styles of East Coast and West Coast rap. In 1999 Eminem described how he blended the two styles:

> **"[I take] a little from the east, a little from the west. The East Coast is mainly known for lyrics and style, while the West Coast is more known for beats and gangsta rap. I kinda blend it so east meets west halfway, which is the Midwest. To me, that's what it should sound like because that's where I am. I'm in the middle."**

A New Attitude

In 1996 Eminem was working long hours in order to support his family. However he could not give up his dream of being a musician. He noticed that many performers create an alter ego for use on stage. This alternate character could express emotions and opinions that the

Eminem's innovative sound and complex rhyming eventually won him an MTV music award in 1999. Describing himself as neither East Coast nor West Coast, but influenced by both, Eminem's unique style was a big hit with audiences everywhere.

performer himself could not. One day, the idea for a character named Slim Shady popped into Eminem's head. Slim Shady was a bad guy who dealt drugs and thought nothing of killing, raping, and committing other acts of violence. Although Eminem was tough and foul-mouthed, Slim Shady took those characteristics to the extreme.

As he developed his Slim Shady character, Eminem's raps began to change. Previously, others had said he was trying to copy more popular rappers. Now he explored the dark side of his own life—poverty, violence, dead-end jobs, drugs, and homelessness—to create ferocious rhymes and lyrics.

Some of Eminem's old friends were shocked at the raw, violent music he was now performing. However, producer Marky Bass was thrilled that he was back in the music business. He felt Eminem was stronger than ever. The two went back into the studio to record the new sound.

In 1997 Eminem recorded a **demo** for an album called *The Slim Shady EP*. The 10 songs on the record featured his unique, rapid-fire style of rapping combined with lyrics that were much darker than those he had previously recorded. In his Slim Shady character, Eminem rapped about murder, rape, and dealing and using drugs.

Fans responded positively to Eminem's new style. Although he was still far from a popular recording artist, he became well known in the underground rap scene. The fact that Eminem was white helped him stand out, and he began to attract national attention.

Welcome to Aftermath

Eminem sent *The Slim Shady EP* to several record companies, hoping someone would sign him to a major label. According to MTV, Jimmy Iovine, head of Interscope Records, one of the most popular and prestigious rap labels, saw Eminem win second place in a contest called the 1997 Rap Olympics and asked him for a demo. Iovine was intrigued by Eminem's fresh sound, so he passed the demo along to Dr. Dre, an influential rapper and producer. Dre also liked what he heard, and he signed Eminem to his record label, Aftermath Entertainment, which was affiliated with Interscope. Together, Dr. Dre and Eminem produced *The Slim Shady LP*.

The two worked well together, and their positive energy was clear in the finished product. *The Slim Shady LP* was released in 1999 and went **triple platinum** by the end of the year. One of the songs, "My Name Is,"

Eminem's drive to make it in the music world fueled his album *The Slim Shady EP*, recorded with the help of Marky Bass. Here, Eminem performs before a live audience at a small show in Michigan during 1997, wearing a Slim Shady t-shirt.

became a huge hit single. In 2000 *The Slim Shady LP* won a Grammy award as the Best Rap Album of the year.

Also in 1999 Eminem's personal life saw positive developments. He and Kim had been broken up for some time, but they were back together again. And in 1999 the two got married.

Influential rapper and producer Dr. Dre performs with Eminem at the opening of the Experience Music Project in Seattle, Washington. The project is an interactive museum of music designed to teach people about the creative process in American music.

Controversy

The Slim Shady LP brought Eminem national fame. However, the album also brought a great deal of controversy. Many people were shocked at Eminem's violent lyrics, especially those that described brutality against women. One of the most controversial songs on the album was "97 Bonnie and Clyde." In this song, he talks about taking a ride with his baby daughter to dispose of his wife's corpse.

In his own defense, Eminem insisted that Slim Shady was just a character. Just as an author can create a character who does bad things, he had created the character of a young man who had no morals and committed acts of violence. Additionally, he felt that Slim Shady was a humorous character. Many music critics agreed. In his book *Whatever You Say I Am*, *Rolling Stone* writer Anthony Bozza compares Slim Shady to a type of literary character known as The Fool. Bozza writes:

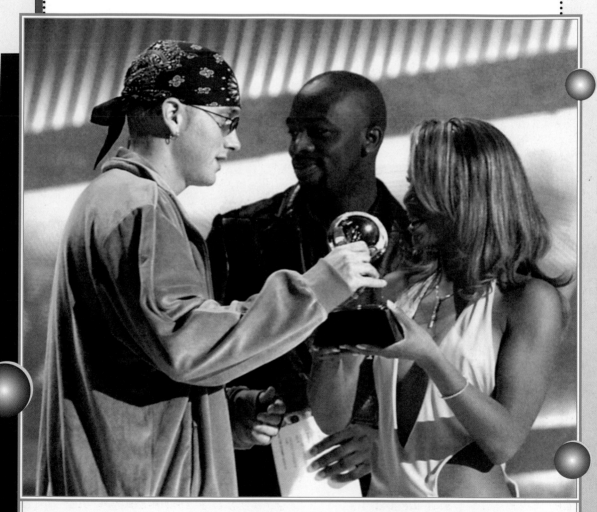

Rapper Eminem accepts his award for Best Rap Album at the 43rd Grammy Awards. He has won nine Grammy awards over the course of his career, including three in the category of Best Rap Album.

"[The Fool] is the character who darts across the plot to tip the audience to truths unseen by the other characters. The Fool is sly, smarter than he lets on, and concealed by his comedy. He may annoy or illuminate, but he won't be ignored."

The Marshall Mathers LP

Eminem did not let the controversy around his lyrics slow him down. In fact, all the media attention made him more popular among his fans and music critics. Eminem's next album, *The Marshall Mathers LP*, was released in 2000, and it was even more popular than *The Slim Shady LP* had been. The album quickly sold 2 million copies. One song, "The Real Slim Shady," became a hit single. *The Marshall Mathers LP* was nominated for a Grammy for Album of the Year. Although it did not win that award, it was chosen as Best Rap Album, and "The Real Slim Shady" won the award for Best Rap Solo Performance.

As with *The Slim Shady LP*, *The Marshall Mathers LP* caused a tremendous amount of controversy. Once again, Eminem described shocking violence against women. One song was called "Kill You" and talked about Eminem raping his mother. Another song, "Kim," described a fight between Eminem and his wife that ended with him cutting her throat.

Gay rights advocates also had problems with the album because Eminem often used the insulting word "faggot" and bashed homosexuals in his lyrics. A major gay rights organization called GLAAD organized a boycott of the Grammy Awards to protest Eminem's nomination. Eminem insisted that he had nothing against homosexuals and that his raps were fictional stories. He also said that he used the offensive word because many teenagers did, without specifically intending to insult gay people. In response to the GLAAD boycott, Eminem sang his song "Stan" onstage during the ceremony with homosexual musician Elton John. The performance ended with a hug between the two men, but Eminem's critics were not impressed.

Eminem's Appeal

Although fans and music critics enjoyed Eminem's energetic style of rapping, his style was not the only reason he became so successful. A big reason for his popularity was the quality of his lyrics; they stood out

Demonstrators from the gay rights group GLAAD rally outside the 2001 Grammy Awards to protest Eminem's nomination. They felt that his use of offensive language and the hateful attitude expressed toward gays in his songs should not be rewarded.

from other rap offerings. At the time, most hip-hop artists bragged about having lots of money and jewelry (called "bling"). Other popular topics were going to parties and having sex with many different women.

Eminem had a different approach. He focused on personal problems and presented a grittier view of life. His raps were graphic, honest, and filled with images of his rough childhood, his difficult relationships with his mother and his wife, his drug use, his love for his daughter, his anger, and his sense of **alienation** from the world around him.

Fans reach out to touch Eminem as he performs live at the Palladium in Worcester, Massachusetts. Although rap was once a music genre confined to black ghettos, today young people of every ethnic background can connect with Eminem's sense of anger and alienation.

Eminem's lyrics struck a chord with many listeners. In 2001 pop culture critic Mim Udovitch described his appeal in a *New York Times* article:

> **"There are millions who are just like him, who cuss like him . . . dress like him, walk, talk, and act like him, and, based on his sales, feel like him. That is: they feel incredible anger. They may be, as he was, children of welfare families, growing up to work for minimum wages. . . . But that these millions exist, and that Eminem speaks for them, is probably what is both truly subversive and truly threatening about his success."**

Eminem had achieved his dream. He was at the top of the hip-hop world and an important figure in pop culture. He had enough money to support his family and make sure his daughter would not have the rough-and-tumble childhood he'd had. However, Eminem's personal life was about to take a dangerous turn.

Eminem shows off the tattoo on his arm, which is a portrait of his daughter, Hailie. A happy home life with his beloved daughter was not in Eminem's future, however, as he and Kim began fighting soon after their marriage.

4

The Troubles in Eminem's World

For many years Eminem had rapped about family members, especially his mother and his wife. These songs were almost always negative and violent, and they captured everyone's attention with their brutality. Beginning in 1999 family problems became an even bigger feature of Eminem's life and affected his career and his music.

Several of Eminem's songs criticized his mother, Debbie. In his hit song "My Name Is," he rapped about his mother's drug use, saying, "Ninety-nine percent of my life I was lied to. I just found out my mom does more dope than I do." He also accused Debbie in numerous interviews of abusing prescription drugs.

In September 1999 Debbie filed a lawsuit against her son. She claimed he had ruined her character and demanded $10 million in damages. In typical fashion Eminem used the lawsuit as inspiration for another song. In "Marshall Mathers" on *The Marshall Mathers LP*, he talked about his "mom suing for $10 million. She must want a dollar for every pill I been stealin'." He said, "where the f--- you think I picked up the habit? All I had to do was go in her room and lift up a mattress."

Debbie also complained that Eminem was ignoring his family. Even though the rapper and his wife and daughter were living in a big, beautiful house, Debbie said he had not kept his promise to pay for her mobile home, which the bank eventually took away from her. Additionally, she said that while Kim had an expensive new car, Eminem's uncle (Debbie's brother Nelson) had to drive an old car with more than 200,000 miles on it. Although these claims were not part of the lawsuit, Debbie did not hesitate to talk to reporters and spread the word that Eminem was refusing to help his impoverished family by sharing his money. Eminem's aunt and uncle also sued the rapper, claiming that he had not fulfilled a promise to pay their property taxes and that, because of this, they were being evicted from their home.

Eminem and Debbie finally settled their lawsuit in 2001. Eminem paid his mother $25,000. However, by court order, almost all of the money went to Debbie's lawyers, and she ended up with less than $2,000.

Troubles with Kim

In 1999 Eminem had married his long-time girlfriend Kim Scott. He was thrilled to finally be able to live full-time with their daughter, Hailie. In addition, Kim and Eminem had full custody of Kim's niece, Alaina. Alaina was the daughter of Kim's twin sister, but she had lived with her aunt and uncle from the time she was born. The relationship between Eminem and Kim had always been rocky, but after their marriage the two soon developed serious problems.

In June 2000 Eminem got into trouble with the law. He was arrested after he pulled a gun on Douglas Dail, a member of rap group Insane Clown Posse. Eminem and Insane Clown Posse had long been rivals.

The very next day Eminem and his gun were again in the news. On June 4, 2000, Eminem saw his wife kiss another man outside the Hot Rocks Café in Warren, Michigan. The man was John Guerra, a **bouncer** at Hot Rocks and a friend of Kim's. Although Kim said the kiss was nothing serious, Eminem was furious. He pulled out an empty 9mm semi-automatic weapon, threatened Guerra, and then pistol-whipped him. Once again, Eminem was arrested, this time for assault and weapons possession. In 2001 the rapper pled guilty to the weapons charges in both cases. In exchange the assault charges were

Kim and Eminem's relationship had always been a difficult one, but things became worse after their marriage. Drugs have contributed to their problems. In 2001 Kim Mathers was arrested for cocaine possession; she later spent a year in prison.

dropped. Eminem paid $100,000 in damages and was put on **probation** for two years.

Kim was angry with Eminem over the incident and upset about the way her life was going. She was so depressed that suicide seemed like the only way out. On July 7, 2000, she tried to kill herself by cutting her wrists. Eminem was performing and not at home at the time, but Kim's mother was in the house. She found her bleeding daughter and called 911 for help. Paramedics and police quickly arrived, and Kim's suicide attempt failed.

Eminem expresses his regrets about the incident with John Guerra to reporters in a courtroom in April 2001. He was placed on two years' probation. The probation had positive aspects, as it forced the rapper to end his drug use.

Although Kim's life was saved, her marriage was beyond repair. A few months after Kim's suicide attempt, Eminem filed for divorce. Although he and Kim got back together later that year, their reunion did not last long. The couple's divorce became final in October 2001.

Kim's troubles did not end with the divorce. In 2003 she was sentenced to two years' probation for possessing cocaine and running from the police. In 2004, while still on probation, she failed a drug test and was sent to jail for 30 days.

Father Figure

After their divorce Kim and Eminem were granted joint custody of Hailie, who was then almost six years old. However, Kim's drug troubles and arrests meant that she was unable to care for her daughter, and the little girl ended up spending most of her time with her father. Kim's niece, Alaina, also lived full-time with Eminem.

The rapper took his role as a father very seriously. "It's no secret what's been going on over the past year with my ex-wife," he told *Rolling Stone* in 2004. "With her being on the run from the cops I really had no choice but to just step up to the plate." He told the interviewer that he had simple goals as a parent:

> **"Teach them right from wrong as best I can, try not to lose my temper, try to set guidelines and rules and boundaries. Never lay a hand on them. Let them know it's not right for a man to ever lay his hands on a female. Despite what people may think of me and what I say in my songs . . . I'm tryin' to teach them and make them learn from my mistakes. . . . I'm not sayin' I'm the perfect father, but the most important thing is to be there for my kids and raise them the right way."**

Eminem also took over caring for his younger half-brother, Nathan. The rapper had been devastated when the state social services agency had taken Nathan away from Debbie and placed him in a foster home. At the time Eminem was struggling financially and did not have a stable home life himself, so he was unable to take in the boy. Eminem made a vow to change the situation. "I always said if I ever get in a position to take him, I would take him," Eminem said. "I watched him when he was in the foster home. The same thing that had happened in my life was happening in his. It was like, 'Man, if I get in position, I'm gonna stop this.' And I got in position and did."

Being on probation after his arrests in 2000 was a blessing in disguise for Eminem, because it helped him settle down. Before that he had taken drugs, especially amphetamines ("uppers"), barbiturates ("downers"), and Ecstasy. However, part of his probation involved taking random drug tests, so he had to stop using drugs in order to stay out of prison. He also worked to keep his temper in check. "I chilled out a lot as far as the drinking and the drugs and all that stuff," he told *Rolling Stone*. "Just chillin' out on that made me see things a lot clearer and learn to rationalize a lot more. Sobering up, becoming an adult."

By 2002 Eminem had put most of his legal and personal problems behind him. It was time to get back to his career. This time, music would not be the only focus of his attention.

Eminem accepts the MTV Video Music award for Video of the Year in 2002. It was a year of great accomplishments, as *8 Mile* was also released that year and would go on to win Eminem an Oscar.

5

New Horizons

Eminem released his next album, *The Eminem Show*, in the summer of 2002. Like his previous albums, the songs on *The Eminem Show* were filled with insults. In his songs Eminem delivered harsh criticisms of so-called "boy bands," such as the popular group *NSYNC, as well as alternative musicians like Limp Bizkit and Moby.

Eminem also took aim at Lynne Cheney, wife of vice president Dick Cheney. In 2000 Lynne Cheney had appeared before a Senate committee that was discussing complaints that the entertainment industry was deliberately targeting children with violent and sexually explicit lyrics. Cheney agreed with this view. Her testimony singled out Eminem as a big part of the problem. She complained that Eminem's raps promoted "violence of the most degrading kind against women" and that "he has taken hatred of women and depictions of degrading and violating them to new levels." As he so often did, Eminem took his revenge against Mrs. Cheney by insulting her through his music.

Despite the criticisms and insults cast at others, *The Eminem Show* was much less violent and brutal than the rapper's previous albums had been. Instead, the rapper focused more on his troubled relationship with Kim, his love for his daughter, and his position in the hip-hop community.

The Silver Screen

Although Eminem released an album during 2002, most of the attention he received that year was for his movie *8 Mile*. The film was a loosely autobiographical look at a white Detroit rapper's life, with Eminem playing the starring role. His character, Jimmy "Rabbit" Smith Jr., is a poor high school dropout who lives with his alcoholic mother and beloved younger sister. The family lives on 8 Mile Road, a real Detroit street which Eminem has described as "the borderline of what separates suburb from city." Jimmy is white, but like his black friends, he dreams of achieving stardom as a rapper.

Although the movie featured Eminem's music and was based on his experiences as a battle rapper, it was definitely not a musical. *8 Mile* was a serious drama. Rather than build a movie around Eminem's songs, the movie was built around his life. He wanted the film to be realistic and made sure every detail was correct. His biggest fear was that the story would seem phony.

8 Mile was directed by Curtis Hanson, who had won praise as the director of *L.A. Confidential* and *Wonder Boys*. Hanson refused to take on the film until he was sure that Eminem was serious about his acting. The director recognized the importance of hip-hop culture to many young people. "No one's helping kids figure out where they're going—not just in the inner cities but in the suburbs," Hanson said. "Hip-hop comes out of that. It is a voice for people who don't have another voice."

Eminem agreed that it was important to show hip-hop's social relevance. He also wanted to explain his own love of rap and how he had relied on it to survive a difficult **adolescence**. "I wanted to make a movie that every kid who went through anything similar to this can relate to," the rapper said. "This was my whole life. If I lost a battle at the hip-hop shop when I was coming up, it literally tore me apart inside."

8 Mile did well at the box office. The movie received mostly positive reviews, and Eminem was complimented for his acting. The film's

**Director Curtis Hanson speaks with Eminem on the set of
8 Mile. Hanson, who had previously directed such films as
L.A. Confidential and *The Hand That Rocks the Cradle*, felt
8 Mile would give him the chance to explore a hidden portion
of society.**

music was also a success. The soundtrack was number one on the
U.S. album charts for four weeks. Eminem also won an Academy Award
for the song "Lose Yourself," which was featured in the movie. "Lose
Yourself" became the first rap song to ever win an Academy Award.

Encore to Controversy

In 2004 Eminem released the album *Encore*. It didn't take long for
the songs on the album to put him in the spotlight once more. In
October Eminem released the single and video for "Just Lose It."
The song's title was a **parody** of Michael Jackson's lyric "just beat it"
from his 1983 hit song "Beat It." The video for the song also parodied
Jackson, focusing on the entertainer's legal troubles because of child
molestation charges, his numerous plastic surgeries, and even an

incident during the 1980s when Jackson's hair caught fire while he was filming a commercial for Pepsi.

One week after the song and video were released, Michael Jackson himself called a Los Angeles radio show hosted by black comedian Steve Harvey to complain about the content of the video. Many other black entertainers spoke out against "Just Lose It," as did members of Jackson's family. Stevie Wonder, one of the most respected African-American

Eminem performs at the 2004 MTV Europe Music Awards in Rome. With him onstage were 68 children under the age of 10, brought for his performance of "Just Lose It," a parody of Michael Jackson that references his child molestation cases.

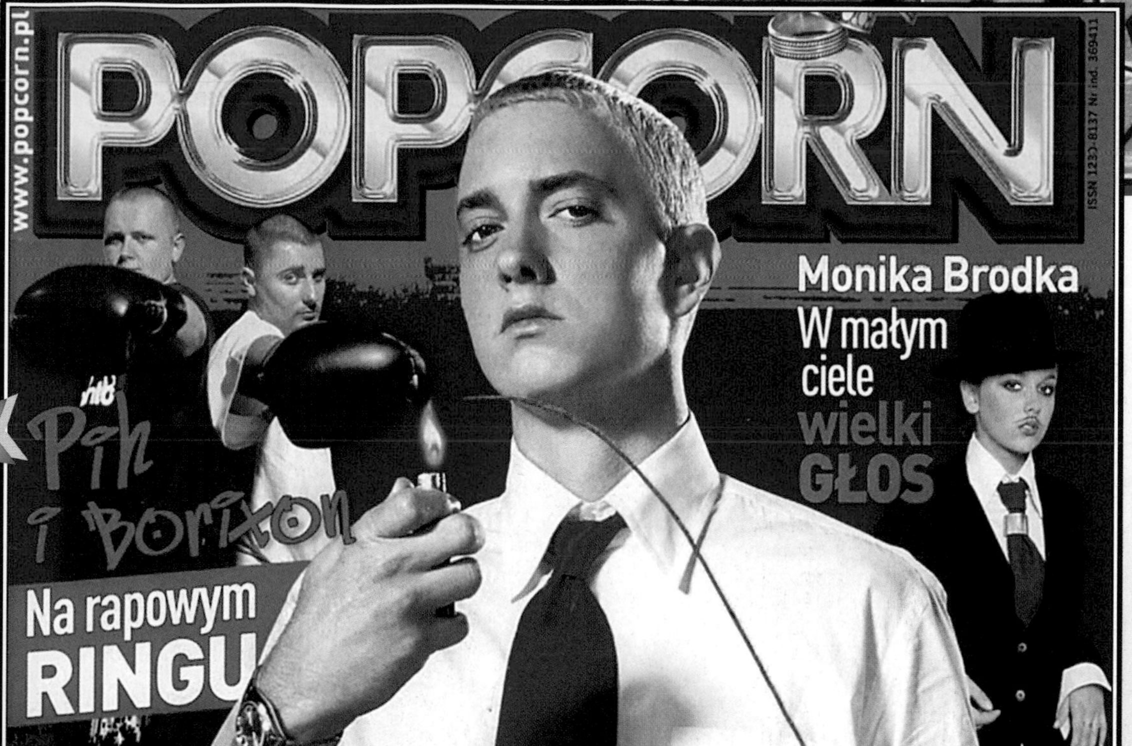

www.popcorn.pl

ISSN 1230-8137 Nr ind. 369411

POPCORN

Monika Brodka
W małym
ciele
wielki
GŁOS

Pih
i Borixon

Na rapowym
RINGU

4 POSTERY

Eminem
Wściekły

This cover of the Polish magazine *Popcorn* depicts Eminem lighting a stick of dynamite, perhaps a reference to the firestorms his music usually incites. In 2004 he was criticized for his parody of Michael Jackson, which many people in the entertainment industry did not appreciate.

artists of the past 50 years, scolded Eminem for "kicking a man while he's down." Steve Harvey added that "Eminem has lost his ghetto pass," and expressed disappointment about Eminem's statements. Harvey also urged the video-music networks MTV and VH1 to stop playing the video, but the cable channels refused. Instead, "Just Lose It" became one of the most popular videos on MTV. Eminem defended his song, pointing out that he did not do anything in the video that Jackson himself had not admitted to doing.

The controversy became even more troublesome when Black Entertainment Television (BET), a cable channel that predominantly airs programming directed at African Americans, refused to air the video for "Just Lose It" because it was so disrespectful to Jackson. Their position was hailed by many in the black community. One outspoken supporter of BET's video ban was Benzino, the chief executive officer of the popular African-American magazine *The Source*. Benzino had disliked Eminem for a long time and used this incident to criticize the rapper again:

> **"For too long, influential people in the hip-hop community have stood by Eminem while he has made a mockery of the culture that inspires and motivates our young people to achieve and be proud of their black heritage. We as the leaders in the hip-hop community and music industry need to step up and realize that Eminem's lyrics and actions are tearing down [our] very culture. . . . I urge all members of hip-hop to come out and support Jackson, one of the most important cultural icons of our time."**

The outcry against "Just Lose It" did not help *Encore*'s record sales. Although by most standards the album was successful, selling 4.7 million copies, it fell far below the sales of Eminem's previous album. Critics called the album's production "bland" and said Eminem's flow (the rhythm and pacing of his raps) sounded lazy.

Political Outcries

Eminem's view of the world broadened in 2004. For the first time, he began rapping about political issues. On October 26, 2004, just one week before the U.S. presidential election, Eminem released a video

Eminem performs at the Shady National Convention 2004, a televised concert event spoofing political conventions, which he organized to promote his new CD, *Encore*. At the convention he also announced the debut of his new radio station, Shade 45, on Sirius Radio.

for his song "Mosh" on the Internet. The song spoke out strongly against president George W. Bush, calling him "a weapon of mass destruction" because of his role in the war against Iraq. The video encouraged viewers to vote in the upcoming election, clearly hoping they would elect Bush's opponent, John Kerry. After Bush won the election, the ending of the video was changed to show protesters invading the White House while President Bush gave a speech.

"Mosh" was not the first time Eminem had spoken out against President Bush, although it was the first public statement. Late in 2003 an unreleased Eminem song called "We As Americans" had been leaked onto the Internet. The lyrics included the line, "I'd rather see the president dead."

Eminem also spoke out against the president's decision to invade Iraq during a 2004 *Rolling Stone* interview. "I think he started a mess," the rapper said. "America is the best country there is, the best country to live in. But he . . . could run our country into the ground. . . . And we got young people over there dyin', kids in their teens, early twenties, who should have futures ahead of them."

A Tour Cut Short

In the summer of 2005, Eminem began his first tour in three years. After numerous successful dates in the United States, the tour was supposed to move on to Europe. However, Eminem shocked his fans when he canceled that part of the tour. The rapper had been abusing a brand of sleeping pills called Ambien, and he decided to enter a **rehabilitation** program to break his **addiction**.

In 2005 rumors began to spread that perhaps Eminem was tired of being a rapper. These rumors suggested that he was more interested in working on the production side of music-making. However, Eminem denied the rumors.

Although Eminem had previously abused illegal drugs such as amphetamines, barbiturates, and marijuana, he had stopped using those after he was put on probation for assault in 2000. However, in the years that followed, he had become **dependent** on prescription medicines, which can be just as dangerous as illegal drugs. The rapper spent a short time in rehab and seemed to have broken that destructive habit.

A Real Curtain Call?

In 2005 rumors began to swirl around Eminem's future. Word had it that he was about to retire from rap. In July 2005 Eminem's hometown newspaper, the *Detroit Free Press*, published a story saying that he would no longer perform as a solo artist. Instead, they said, he would become a record producer for other rappers.

Eminem denied these rumors while on his U.S. tour. However, his actions seemed to suggest that there might be some truth to them. In December 2005 the rapper released the album *Curtain Call*. The title alone seemed to suggest that Eminem was thinking of leaving the music industry. Even more intriguing was a song on the album called "When I'm Gone." In this song Eminem talks about murdering Slim Shady, the violent, foul-mouthed character who made him famous. The song includes the lyrics "Find a gun on the ground, cock it, put it to my brain, scream 'Die Shady!' and pop it."

Eminem had also talked about taking a break from his rap career to explore other areas, such as acting and producing. His last two albums have not sold nearly as well as his first two, so moving on to a new phase in his career seems only natural.

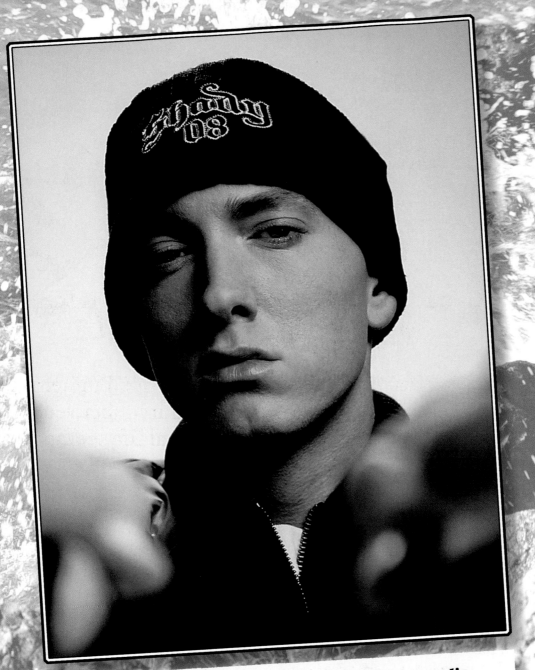

Eminem's personal life was often as great a media spectacle as his controversial music. His relationship with Kim was wild and tumultuous, ending eventually in divorce. In the midst of that break-up, one of Eminem's close friends died violently.

6

Outside the Music

After all the drama and violence Eminem and his family had endured between 1999 and 2003, his personal life seemed to settle down considerably during 2005. That year brought big and surprising changes to Eminem's home life. His actions also showed the world that Eminem was a man who had matured from his early days as a rapper.

In a 2004 *Rolling Stone* interview, Eminem had said that the romantic side of his relationship with Kim was "pretty much out the window," but that the two still had to show each other respect because of their daughter. In that same interview, Eminem said that Kim was "a woman who's been a part of my life since I can remember." Many people were surprised in December 2005 when Eminem told an interviewer for a Detroit radio station that he and his ex-wife had gotten back together. Just one month later, on January 14, 2006, Eminem and Kim remarried.

The Mathers family was larger than ever before. In addition to Hailie, Alaina, and Nathan, the new family also included Kim's two-year-old daughter Whitney. She had given birth to Whitney while she and Eminem were divorced. Even though he was not the girl's biological father, Eminem cared for Whitney and planned to adopt her.

Troubles and Tragedy

Unfortunately, Eminem's happiness did not last long. In early April 2006, less than three months after getting married again, Eminem filed for divorce. Eminem did not provide details about why the couple split again, but a few days later in a radio interview, Kim said the divorce was a surprise and blamed their breakup on Eminem's continuing addiction to prescription drugs. "I was hoping we could get counseling and work it out," she said. "I got an attorney at the door instead."

Less than a week later, Eminem was hit by another blow. His best friend Deshaun Holton, a rapper who was known by the name Proof, was killed in a gunfight at a Detroit nightclub. Proof had rapped with Eminem in the group D12 and had also served as best man at Eminem's January 2006 wedding. Eminem was devastated by the sudden loss of his friend. "Proof and I were brothers," he said. "He pushed me to become who I am. Without Proof's guidance and encouragement, there would have been a Marshall Mathers, but probably not an Eminem and certainly never a Slim Shady."

Not Just a Recording Artist

In addition to his career as a rapper, Eminem has had several other business interests. In 2000 he helped create Shady Records and continues to work as owner of the label. Shady Records operates under the umbrella of Aftermath Entertainment, which is owned by rap producer and performer Dr. Dre. Shady Records's most famous artist is 50 Cent. The superstar rapper was originally signed to both Shady Records and Aftermath Entertainment in a joint venture. Other artists on the label include Atlanta rappers Bobby Creekwater and Stat Quo and Detroit rapper Obie Trice.

Eminem has also produced many hip-hop songs. He produced several songs on 50 Cent's best-selling albums *Get Rich or Die Tryin'* and *The Massacre*. He has also produced songs for The Game, Jay-Z, Lloyd Banks, and Xzibit, as well as D12. In addition, Eminem produced most of the tracks on his album *The Eminem Show* and co-produced *Encore* with Dr. Dre. Eminem also produced *Loyal to the Game* by Tupac Shakur, which was the 12th album released under Tupac's name after his murder.

Rapper Proof, actor Mekhi Phifer, and rapper Eminem perform at the *8 Mile* DVD release party in Detroit. Proof was a founding member of the rap group D12 and an influential force in Eminem's life. He was shot and killed in April 2006.

Eminem has also branched into satellite radio. On October 28, 2004, he began programming a channel on Sirius Satellite Radio. The hip-hop channel is called Shade 45. Outside of the music industry, Eminem owns a clothing line called Shady Ltd.

Giving Back
Eminem knows how hard it is to grow up poor and disadvantaged. To help young people in similar circumstances, he has donated money

from many of his concerts to support the Boys and Girls Clubs of America. Eminem has also donated concert earnings to the Leary Fire Fighters Foundation. In his hometown of Detroit, the rapper is very involved with helping young people, and he won several awards for his outstanding contributions to youth empowerment and community development during a Detroit event called the Hip-Hop Summit.

Eminem joins NAACP leader Dr. Benjamin Chavis Jr., Def Jam executive Russell Simmons, Detroit mayor Kwame Kilpatrick, and rapper Nas at the 2003 Hip-Hop Summit. Dubbed "The Remix: ReBuilding, ReFocusing, ReInvesting, ReSurgence," the summit offers a forum for rappers to promote positive world changes.

In addition to community and youth programs, Eminem has also reached out to change lives on the national and global stage. He has held political conventions to raise young people's awareness of important national issues and has used his videos to encourage people to vote. In 2003 Eminem donated autographed items for fans to bid on as part of the "Songs of Hope" campaign. This campaign put items up for auction on eBay, with all proceeds benefiting City of Hope. City of Hope is part of the National Cancer Institute; it is dedicated to the prevention and cure of cancer, AIDS, and other serious diseases.

From his earliest days on the music scene, Eminem has had a reputation as an angry, violent young man and a threat to society. However, the rapper is much more than that. He has changed hip-hop music through his clever, inventive raps and honest lyrics. And he tries to change lives by inspiring youth to make a difference and giving them a helping hand when possible. Eminem has come a long way, emerging from a difficult past to create a promising future. And just like his one-of-a-kind raps, Eminem lives his life in his own unique style.

1972 Marshall Bruce Mathers III is born on October 17 in Saint Joseph, Missouri.

1975 Marshall's parents divorce, and Marshall never sees his father again.

1981 Marshall is badly beaten by a bully at school. He is hospitalized and suffers from recurring headaches.

1987 Marshall meets Kimberly Scott.

1995 Marshall and Kim's daughter, Hailie Jade, is born on December 25. Marshall starts working long hours to try to support his family.

1996 Marshall begins performing under the name Eminem. He releases *Infinite*, but no one seems interested in buying his album. Depressed by the musical failure, he tries to kill himself.

1997 Eminem releases *The Slim Shady EP* and wins a hip-hop competition. He is discovered, and Dr. Dre signs him to Aftermath Entertainment.

1999 Eminem releases *The Slim Shady LP*. He finally marries Kim Scott. Debbie, his mother, files a $10 million lawsuit against him.

2000 Eminem releases *The Marshall Mathers LP*. He is arrested twice for weapons possession and assault. Eminem launches his own record label called Shady Records.

2001 Eminem pleads guilty to weapons charges and is put on probation. He and Kim divorce.

2002 Eminem releases *The Eminem Show*. He stars in the auto-biographical movie *8 Mile*. "Lose Yourself," a song from *8 Mile*, is nominated for an Academy Award.

2003 Eminem wins an Academy Award for his song "Lose Yourself."

2004 Eminem releases *Encore* and begins programming a hip-hop channel on Sirius Satellite Radio.

2005 Eminem cancels his European tour to enter rehab for an addiction to sleeping pills. He releases *Curtain Call*, which spurs rumors about an impending retirement.

2006 Eminem and Kim Scott remarry on January 14. Eminem files for divorce again on April 5.

Albums

1996 *Infinite*

1997 *The Slim Shady EP*

1999 *The Slim Shady LP*

2002 *The Marshall Mathers LP*
The Eminem Show
8 Mile Soundtrack

2004 *Encore*

2005 *Curtain Call: The Hits*

Movies

2002 *8 Mile*

Awards

1999 MTV Video Music Award for Best New Artist for "My Name Is"

MTV Europe Music Award for Best Hip-Hop Act

2000 Grammy Award for Best Rap Solo Performance for
"My Name Is"

Grammy Award for Best Rap Album for *The Slim Shady LP*

MTV Europe Music Award for Best Hip-Hop Act and
Best Album for *The Marshall Mathers LP*

MTV Video Music Award for Best Rap Video for
"Forgot About Dre" and Best Male Video and
Best Video for "The Real Slim Shady"

2001 Grammy Award for Best Rap Album for *The Marshall
Mathers LP*, Best Rap Performance by a Duo of Group
for "Forgot About Dre," and Best Rap Solo Performance
for "The Real Slim Shady"

MTV Europe Music Award for Best Hip-Hop Act

2002 MTV Europe Music Award for Best Hip-Hop Act and Best
Album for *The Eminem Show*

MTV Video Music Award for Best Direction, Best Rap Video,
Best Male Video, and Best Video for "Without Me"

2003 Academy Award for Best Song for "Lose Yourself"

American Music Award for Favorite Hip-Hop/R&B Male Artist, Favorite Pop/Rock Male Artist, and Favorite Hip-Hop/R&B Album *for The Eminem Show*

Grammy Award for Best Rap Album for *The Eminem Show* and Best Short Form Music Video for "Without Me"

MTV Europe Music Award for Best Hip-Hop Act

MTV Movie Award for Best Male Performance and Best Breakthrough Performance for *8 Mile*

MTV Video Music Award for Best Video from a Film for "Lose Yourself"

2004 Grammy Award for Best Rap Song for "Lose Yourself" and Best Male Rap Solo Performance

MTV Europe Music Award for Best Hip-Hop Act

2005 American Music Award for Favorite Hip-Hop/R&B Male Artist

Books

Als, Hilton, and Darryl A. Turner, eds. *White Noise: The Eminem Collection.* New York: Thunder's Mouth Press, 2003.

Bozza, Anthony. *Whatever You Say I Am: The Life and Times of Eminem.* New York: Crown Publishers, 2003.

Doggett, Peter. *Eminem: The Complete Guide to His Music.* London: Omnibus Press, 2005.

Eminem. *Angry Blonde.* New York: Regan Books, 2002.

Hasted, Nick. *The Dark Story of Eminem.* London: Omnibus Press, 2003.

Kenyatta, Kelly. *You Forgot About Dre: The Unauthorized Biography of Dr. Dre and Eminem.* Chicago: Busta Books, 2001.

Lane, Stephanie. *Eminem.* San Diego: Lucent Books, 2004.

Legg, Barnaby, and Jim McCarthy. *Eminem In My Skin.* London: Omnibus Press, 2004.

Stubbs, David. *Cleaning Out My Closet: Eminem: The Stories Behind Every Song.* New York: Thunder's Mouth Press, 2003.

Weiner, Chuck. *Eminem Talking.* London: Omnibus Press, 2003.

Web Sites

http://www.allhiphop.com/hiphopnews/

This Web site features news items about Eminem and other hip-hop artists.

http://www.eminem.com

Eminem's official Web site includes news, audio, video, photos, a discography, and links to other sites.

http://www.mtv.com/music/artist/eminem/artist.jhtml

MTV's official Web site includes an Eminem biography, discography, videos, photos, and news.

http://musicbrainz.org/artist/b95ce3ff-3d05-4e87-9e01-c97b66af13d4.html

This Web site includes information about Eminem's music and downloads of his songs.

http://music.yahoo.com/ar-289114-videos--Eminem

You can watch Eminem's music videos on the Yahoo! Launch Web site.

addiction—a physical or psychological dependence on something, such as a drug.

adolescence—the teenage years.

alienation—feeling different and strange from other people.

assault—to attack, threaten, or beat up someone.

bouncer—someone who works as a security guard in a club or bar.

brutal—very cruel and violent.

controversial—something that causes a lot of arguments.

demo—a recording that shows off an artist's skills to a producer or record company executive.

dependent—needing something very badly.

ghetto—a neighborhood that is usually poor where people of the same race or religion live.

graphic—very realistic and detailed.

lyrics—words to a song.

parody—a piece of writing or music that deliberately copies another work in a comic or satirical way.

probation—status granted to a criminal defendant that permits him to serve a sentence outside jail.

producer—a person who is charge of making an album, movie, or television show.

profanity—swearing; bad language.

rehabilitation—a hospital or medical program that helps people overcome addiction.

triple platinum—a record industry designation for an album that has sold more than 3 million copies.

turbulent—wild, confused, or violent.

Joanne Mattern has written more than 200 books for children, including biographies of Celine Dion, Tom Cruise, Bernie Mac, and many sports stars. She specializes in nonfiction and especially enjoys writing about animals, interesting people, and important historical events. Joanne also works in her local library. She lives in New York State with her husband, three daughters, and three cats.

Picture Credits

page

  2: AFP/Timothy A. Clary
  8: Reuters/Robert Galbraith
 11: AFP/Timothy A. Clary
 12: UPI/Laura Cavanaugh
 14: Zuma/Tony Bock/Toronto Star
 16: Zuma Archive
 18: Universal Studios/NMI
 19: Universal Studios/NMI
 20: WENN Photos
 22: FPS/NMI
 25: Zuma Press/Nancy Kaszerman
 27: KRT/J. Kyle Keener
 28: KRT/Nancy Stone
 29: AFP/Hector Mata
 31: Michael Germana/UPI

 32: Zuma Press/Steven Tackeff
 34: Tatuni/WSPI
 37: Splash News
 38: KRT/John Collier
 40: AFP/Timothy A. Clary
 43: SHNS/Eli Reed/Universal Studios
 44: S. Lispi/BWPhoto
 45: Michelle Feng/NMI
 47: KRT/Nicolas Khayat
 48: FPS/NMI
 50: PRNewsFoto/NMI
 53: Mandi Wright/Detroit Free Press/KRT
 54: Ramin Talaie/Sipa Press

Front cover: Stephen Trupp/Star Max
Back cover: S. Lispi/BWPhoto